ACTION

DO REVISIT AND **CONTINUE TO** ♥ ♥ ♥ **LEARN** AND **ACT**

DO **BE READY FOR MISTAKES** AND SAYING

DON'T ASSUME

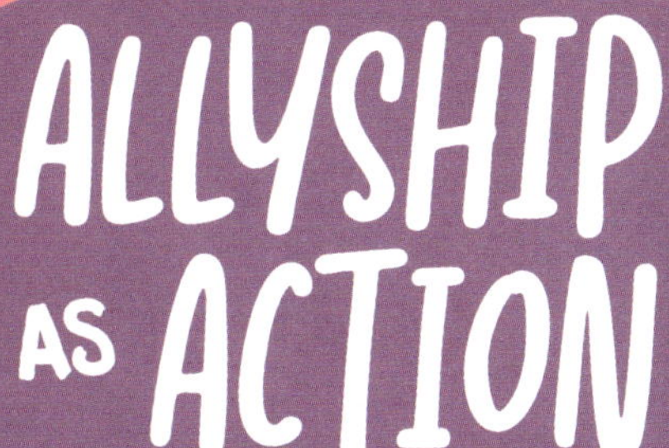

7 Ways to Advocate for Others

TANYA BOTEJU

illustrated by

BITHI SUTRADHAR

ORCA BOOK PUBLISHERS

To everyone willing to engage in this messy, hard work.

CONTENT WARNING: Some of the situations presented here might be challenging to read about, but if you're part of the dominant group presented in a particular situation, that's kind of the point! If you're in a marginalized group that appears in a situation, you may feel sad, angry or uncomfortable, especially if you've had a similar experience. I've tried to stay away from anything explicit or potentially harmful, but make sure you have someone you can talk with about these feelings, just in case.

Published in Canada and the United States in 2025 by Orca Book Publishers.

Library and Archives Canada Cataloguing in Publication
Title: Allyship as action : 7 ways to advocate for others / Tanya Boteju ; illustrated by Bithi Sutradhar.
Names: Boteju, Tanya, author | Sutradhar, Bithi, illustrator.
Description: Series statement: Orca take action ; 1 | Includes bibliographical references and index.
Identifiers: Canadiana (print) 2024048505X | Canadiana (ebook) 20240485068 | ISBN 9781459840478 (hardcover) | ISBN 9781459840485 (PDF) | ISBN 9781459840492 (EPUB)
Subjects: LCSH: Allyship—Juvenile literature. | LCSH: Solidarity—Juvenile literature.
Classification: LCC HM717 .B65 2025 | DDC j302/.14—dc23

Library of Congress Control Number: 2024947385

Summary: Part of the nonfiction Orca Take Action series for middle-grade readers, this illustrated book introduces young readers to what it means to be an ally and realistic actions they can take to practice allyship in their own lives.

Orca Book Publishers is committed to reducing the consumption of nonrenewable resources in the production of our books. We make every effort to use materials that support a sustainable future.

Orca Book Publishers gratefully acknowledges the support for its publishing programs provided by the following agencies: the Government of Canada, the Canada Council for the Arts and the Province of British Columbia through the BC Arts Council and the Book Publishing Tax Credit.

Edited by Kirstie Hudson.
Design by Troy Cunningham.

Printed and bound in Canada.

28 27 26 25 • 2 3 4 5

CERTIFIED CANADIAN PUBLISHER

CONTENTS

WELCOME

Hello! I'm so happy to see you here because it probably means you're someone who cares about other people and wants to learn more about how to care for others in meaningful ways. Reading this book is a great step toward that goal. I appreciate your willingness to learn.

Allyship is a complicated matter, so be prepared to get a little messy here. My own journey to being an ally to others hasn't been easy or clear. I've made mistakes. I can always do more. I'm still learning, and sometimes that learning is hard. But don't let the complications and mess stop you from reading on. Anything worthwhile is going to take some work. I know you have what it takes to be a great ally—if you're willing to keep an open mind, try some new things and keep going, even when it's hard.

This book isn't meant to be the final word on allyship. It's a piece of a much bigger puzzle. But you may never get the complete picture, because conversations about allyship can change and evolve, and there are so many ways to be an ally. Don't expect to be a perfect ally to everyone—that's impossible! But you can learn to be a better ally to more people. This book is meant to help you do that in practical and—hopefully—accessible ways. I hope this book gives you tools to be a better ally, sparks new questions for further learning, and inspires you to take action.

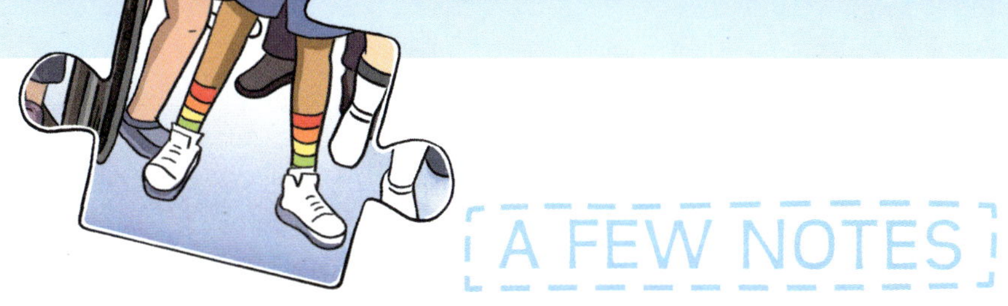

A FEW NOTES

While I feel I have some knowledge to contribute to the area of allyship, I know that there are many, many people who have made and are making huge contributions as well. Some of those people and organizations can be found in the Resources section of this book.

If you really want to get the most out of this book, I recommend reading it with others so you can discuss the issues and hear different perspectives. It's good to get outside of our own brains sometimes!

Even though we are mainly considering individual allyship in this book, just know that many injustices are built into *systems* (like educational institutions, legal systems, etc.). That means that the project of allyship and creating justice for all is bigger than any one person.

We all know books are magical, but know that allyship will require you to go beyond this book toward action. We can read books on every topic, but if we're not putting our learning into actions and practice, we're not making the impact we could.

EXTRA-SPECIAL NOTE: I think you're awesome for being here. Now let's dig in!

QUALITIES OF AN ALLY

1. ALLIES ARE WILLING TO CONTINUALLY REFLECT, LISTEN AND LEARN.
2. ALLIES KNOW THAT ALLYSHIP REQUIRES ACTION.
3. ALLIES UNDERSTAND THAT ALLYSHIP ISN'T EASY OR COMFORTABLE, YET ARE UP FOR THE CHALLENGE.

Allies Are Willing to Continually Reflect, Listen and Learn

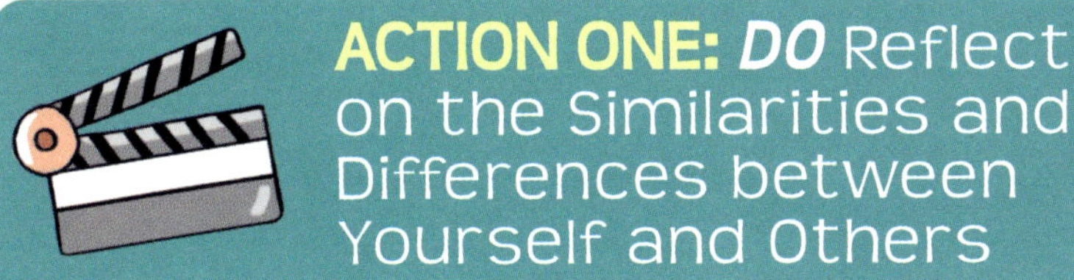

ACTION ONE: *DO* Reflect on the Similarities and Differences between Yourself and Others

THE SITUATION: Think More, Act Better

Jesse walks to the bathroom between band performances at a concert. A lot of other people have also gone to the bathroom, and because the lineup is very long, all of the eight stalls are in use, including the accessible stall (a stall for people with disabilities). Jesse stands in line like everyone else, and when it's their turn, the next open stall happens to be the accessible stall. Jesse thinks nothing of it as they use this stall, then wash their hands and leave. As they leave, they notice someone waiting in line who is using a wheelchair.

When someone has privilege, they have an advantage over others in some way, and this advantage is often supported by the places and people around them. In this scenario, Jesse has able-bodied privilege. Jesse can easily walk from their seat to the bathroom, stand in line for a few minutes, use any of the stalls in the bathroom, then walk out again.

Jesse doesn't even think about how easy this is because they're used to it—most public spaces are set up in a way that meets the needs of able-bodied people.

However, most buildings and spaces are not set up to meet the needs of people with disabilities. And many people who are able-bodied don't automatically think about how their actions or inaction might affect people with disabilities. Part of being privileged is not always considering how people who don't have the same privilege experience things. The world is built for us in certain ways, so we might not even think about how it's unfair for others.

So let's think about it now—what might this situation be like for someone with a disability?

WHAT COULD JESSE DO DIFFERENTLY NEXT TIME?

- Look around to see if there might be someone who needs the accessible stall, including a person with children, an older person with mobility issues or a person with an injury.
- Ask if anyone needs to go ahead of them in line or use the accessible stall.
- Choose a non-accessible stall whenever possible.
- Consider how other spaces they use in the future might be made more accessible and then seek out people who could help them advocate for any changes that need to be made. What if *all* stalls were accessible?

Privilege:

An unearned advantage given to some people but not all. Privileges are based on factors such as race, gender, sexuality, class and more. Unfair advantages we might have in society can include things like having a safe home, seeing our identities represented consistently in the media or feeling a sense of belonging in most places we go. Having privilege doesn't make you a bad person, but it's important to be able to recognize our privilege and use it to help others who face unfair disadvantages.

Marginalized:

Treated as "less than" by society due to race, religion, age, gender, etc.

Allyship:

Active and consistent effort by someone to understand, empower and support people who might not have the same rights and freedoms as they themselves have.

A DIFFERENT KIND of EXPERIENCE

Of course, every individual is different, but someone with a disability may not find it easy to make their way to the bathroom. It may take them a little longer, they may need to wait for an elevator, they may have a hard time maneuvering around other people. Once they get to the bathroom, they may have to wait in line because the accessible stall is being used by everyone—able-bodied and disabled alike. They may not feel like they can ask to move ahead in the line to use the accessible stall, and sometimes those with invisible disabilities—like dizziness caused by a chronic illness—may feel nervous about being seen as able-bodied if they do ask to move ahead.

ASK YOURSELF

What Are the Privileges I Have Based on My Identities?

For example, I have a warm bed to sleep in at night, which helps me get a good night's sleep and pay attention in school. This relates to the privilege of having a home and a family with a certain amount of wealth.

Marginalized means one is valued less due to some aspect of their identity. Being devalued limits that person's ability to function in society. Sometimes marginalization is obvious—excluding a group of people because of the color of their skin, for example, or imprisoning a group because of their religious beliefs. These *are* examples of

marginalization, but sometimes marginalization is less obvious. Not being able to easily access a bathroom stall that suits one's needs is a way of being marginalized. It makes the entire experience harder and less comfortable or convenient for that person. They cannot experience an event or space in the same way as others and may not even want to attend a similar event in the future.

> Being privileged doesn't mean that you are always wrong and people without privilege are always right. It means that there is a good chance you are missing a few very important pieces of the puzzle.

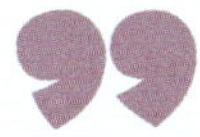

Ijeoma Oluo, author and activist

A main message of this book, as you'll see, is that allyship equals action. In order to be a good ally, we must take action. So how could Jesse have been a better ally in this situation? What actions could they take in the future?

TAKING a CLOSER LOOK at OURSELVES

A first step Jesse can take is noticing, observing and self-reflecting. It's important to understand what our privileges are before we can act in ways that counteract those privileges. Noticing and acknowledging them can be hard, for two main reasons.

First, our privileges are often invisible to us because we're so used to them. For instance, using the stairs in a building is an obvious choice for me because my legs can move up and down stairs easily. I don't even have to think about this because most multilevel buildings have stairs, and I've always been able to use stairs. Buildings that are designed for the way my body functions are the norm for me—like the air I breathe. I expect them to be this way. Because I don't have to think about how to get around a building, I *don't* think about it. So noticing and acknowledging that I have this privilege is harder. Someone needs to point it out to me, or I need to take the time to stop, reflect and consider that this is an area in which I may be privileged.

Second, it might not feel good to admit that we have it easier than others and have privileges that others don't. We might feel surprised or sad or guilty. We might feel angry or resentful if people point out our privileges. But if we're interested in being better allies, understanding where we have privilege is key. If we don't know where we have advantages, how can we use those advantages to support and uplift others? How can we *act* in ways that help make the world less limiting and more successful for all?

We can't. So allyship requires us to ***REFLECT***, ***LISTEN*** and ***LEARN***.

"Acting as an ally means helping and standing with people who don't have the same privileges as you."
Theo, age 12

"Allyship is [...] helping people belong."
Danica, age 12

"When I think of allyship, I think of a warm hug that makes people feel comfortable and at home. I think of all those communities feeling the joy of having someone respect and support them for who they are."
Ellie, age 12

ACTION TWO: *DO* Continually Listen and Learn

THE SITUATION: Learning to Listen

> Change happens by listening and then starting a dialogue with the people who are doing something you don't believe is right.

Jane Goodall,
scientist and activist

Quinn has been doing the work to be a great ally. He's been reflecting on how various aspects of his identity as a white, cisgender male might offer him unearned privileges that others don't have, and he's excited about what he's learning about himself, others and the world around him. Quinn wants to share his reflections and learning, as many of us would.

In Quinn's English class one day, the group is talking about a book they're reading and how the female characters are treated versus the male characters. Here's how the conversation goes:

TEACHER: What do we think about the characterization of male and female characters in this book?

QUINN: The author is a guy, right? So I think he's writing his female characters through his privileged male perspective. That's why the female characters all seem so weak.

RASHIDA: I don't think the female characters are all weak.

QUINN: But they are! Look how much they have to care for the men in their lives. It's like all the women are just there to serve the men. I see that in my own family. When there are dinner parties at our house, all the women are in the kitchen cooking and then cleaning, while all the men are playing cards or whatever. I realize I've been letting my mom and sisters do all the work at these things.

CHARLOTTE: That might be true in your family, but in the book, the female characters actually find empowerment with each other as they do the housework.

RASHIDA: Right. It's like they find community there. They—

QUINN: But at the end of the day, they're still being marginalized, right? Like, they're practically banished to the kitchen and stuff, so how can that be empowering? If they were really empowered, they'd be able to move about freely and do whatever they wanted, whenever they wanted. Right?

How do you feel about Quinn's participation in this conversation?

The most basic of all human needs is the need to understand and be understood. The best way to understand people is to listen to them.

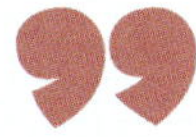

Ralph G. Nichols, educator and author

WORDS to KNOW

Cisgender: Of, being or relating to someone who feels that their gender identity matches the one they were given at birth. The term is often shortened to cis.

Gender Identity: How someone sees their own gender. Someone's gender identity can match or differ from the gender they were labeled with at birth or the gender other people assume they are.

☐ Male
☐ Female
☐ No Gender

what YOU can DO

ACTIONS FOR LISTENING AND LEARNING

- Practice pausing before speaking. Let people who may have experienced marginalization speak before you do.
- Diversify the media you read/watch/listen to. Include perspectives and identities that fall outside of your own.
- Avoid expecting people from marginalized identities to teach you unless they want to.

MAKING ROOM for OTHERS

Did you notice how much space Quinn takes up in his excitement to share his perspective and learning? Quinn has been reflecting on his male privilege—that's clear. And good on him! It's not easy to acknowledge our privileges, as we've already talked about. Plus, he's trying to show that he understands how the male privilege of the author might be playing into the portrayal of women in the text. He's viewing the text through his newfound knowledge and applying it! This is a positive thing.

But in his excitement he's missing out on continued opportunities for listening and learning as well. It's not wrong for him to disagree with his female classmates over the text, but he's not allowing a lot of space for the other perspectives to be shared.

> I learned so much from listening to people. And all I knew was, the only thing I had was honesty and openness.
>
> **Audre Lorde**, activist and author

Unfortunately *and* fortunately, allyship involves continued listening and learning, which can be tricky. How do we share our learning *and* remain open to more learning? How might Quinn have shared his learning here without marginalizing other perspectives?

- Where might I take up more space than I need to? Where can I listen a little more or pause before talking? How could I help create more space for others' perspectives—especially perspectives that might often be marginalized?
- When have I felt like I wasn't being given space to be heard? How did I feel in that moment?
- What questions do I have about allyship? How could I go about finding responses to these questions?

GIVE and TAKE

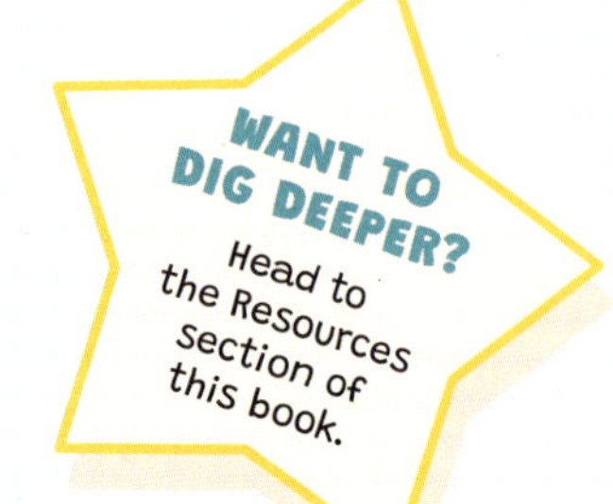

Here are some possibilities:

He could wait to see what others have to offer before offering his own opinions.

He could share briefly and then allow others to share more of their ideas.

He could most definitely let people finish their thoughts before speaking again!

But first he'd need to notice that what he's doing is problematic. This might take more of that self-reflection we talked about earlier. It might require his teacher or another student pointing out how much space he's taking up, and Quinn being open to listening to that feedback and learning from it.

The main point is the reflection, the ***LISTENING***, the ***LEARNING***—it never ends! That might sound a little tiring or overwhelming, and it definitely does take a lot of energy. But these are all opportunities for learning, and if we can see them as such, it might feel a little less overwhelming and a bit more inspiring. That's how I try and look at it, anyway (but I can still get overwhelmed, because I'm only human!).

“Allyship means supporting others and taking time to learn new things.”

Asha, age 12

ACTION THREE: ***DO*** Act in the Moment

THE SITUATION: Tricky Conversations and Daring Actions

Twelve-year-old Hannah is at the dinner table with her family, including several relatives. The occasion is celebratory—it's Nana's birthday! Everyone is having a wonderful time, enjoying the food, conversation and company. But at one point a relative that Hannah really loves—an aunt—expresses some views about transgender people that Hannah finds troubling. This aunt doesn't believe that gender identities should be talked about in schools.

In her classes and through her school's Gender and Sexuality Alliance—a club that celebrates different identities—Hannah has learned about some of the issues her aunt is raising. Her aunt's comments make her feel uncomfortable.

WORDS to KNOW

Transgender: An umbrella term used to describe a person whose gender identity is different from how they were labeled at birth. May be shortened to trans.

Nonbinary: A way of identifying and/or expressing oneself outside the more traditional gender categories of male/masculine and female/feminine.

Hannah herself is cisgender, but she knows people at school who are transgender or nonbinary, some of whom are friends.

But she's one of the youngest people at the table, she really respects her aunt, no one else seems to have a problem with her aunt's comments, and Hannah doesn't feel like she knows enough to say anything. What could she possibly say or do in this situation?

HARD TALK

Allyship can be (and usually is) hard. Being an ally to others will often make us feel uncomfortable, and not everyone will be able to get past that discomfort. But if Hannah feels safe and able, one thing she could do here is speak up for people who might be harmed by her aunt's views, even if she feels uneasy about doing this.

> Do the best you can until you know better. Then when you know better, do better.
>
> **Maya Angelou**, author

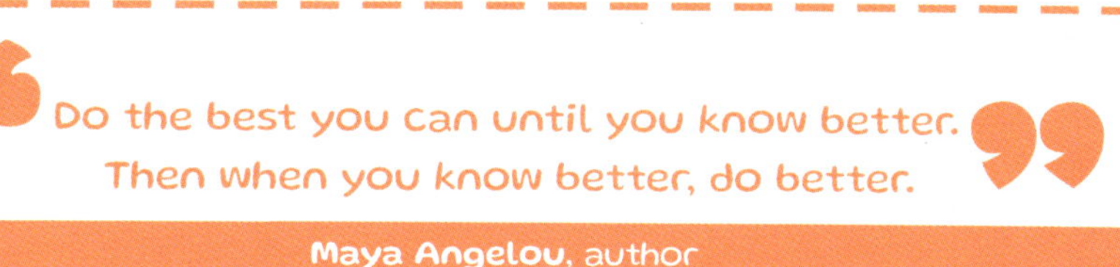

Should Hannah have to explain to her aunt things like gender and sexuality in childhood development, or share statistics about the impact of inclusion and acceptance in schools? No, she shouldn't. At age 12 she might not know much about that stuff anyway (most adults don't either)!

If she knows that what her aunt is saying is different from what she sees her trans and nonbinary friends experiencing at school, she could say

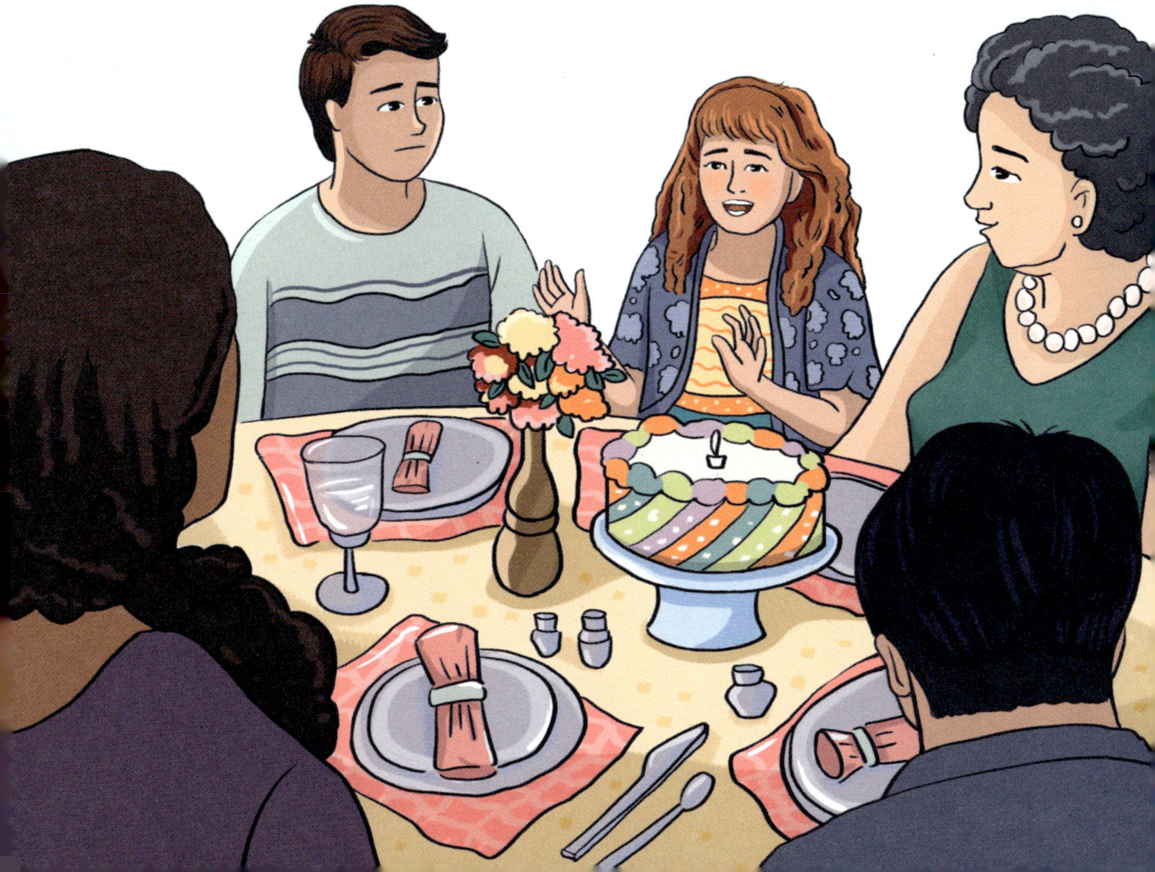

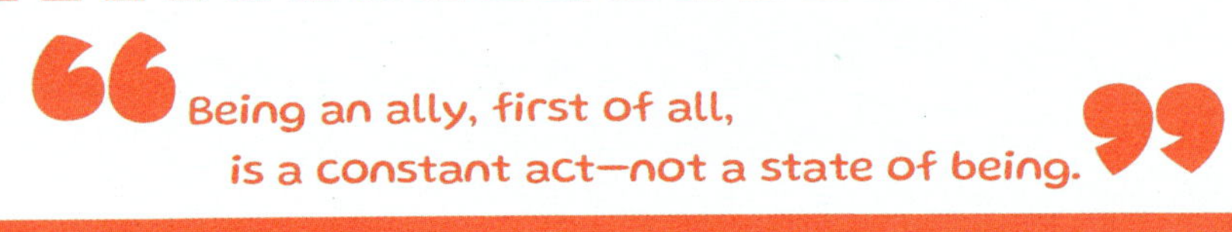

something like: "But Auntie, some of my friends really appreciate learning about these things. Some of them even feel safer because we hear about these things at school. I think it's important too."

What happens if her aunt pushes back a little? What if her aunt does start to talk about childhood development or parents' rights or other things Hannah doesn't feel she knows a lot about? How could Hannah respond then?

SAYING WHAT'S TRUE for YOU

Hannah doesn't need to engage in a full-blown debate with her aunt. In situations like this, it might be best to stick to what you do know and share what is true for you. For instance, Hannah could say, "I don't really know about all of that. I just know that people I care about at school feel safer because we talk about these issues at school. Some of them knew they were trans even when they were younger. And some of their parents don't make them feel safe. So I think it's a good thing if schools are a place where we can talk about these things, even at a younger age."

Hannah's aunt probably won't change her mind. It's fair to say that some adults don't necessarily take young people's opinions all that seriously, unfortunately! But Hannah has spoken up. She's said what she knows to be true. She's acted in allyship with people who need allies to speak up. Maybe someone else at that dinner party hears what she's said and experiences a slight shift in thinking. Maybe her aunt thinks twice about her views. Maybe someone there has a trans child or sister or parent or cousin or friend and is thankful that Hannah said something. Maybe someone at the party is trans or nonbinary but not out yet, and Hannah's words make them feel cared for. We might never know the impact of our actions, but those actions are still key to being a good ally.

"Allyship is standing up for people when they can't do it on their own."
Amelia, age 11

"Allyship, for me, is: 'I will stand by you and make sure you feel loved, cared for and appreciated.'"
Briar, age 12

Performative Ally:
Someone who is more interested in being seen as an ally than actually acting as one and taking action.

Land Acknowledgment:
A statement that recognizes the Traditional, Ancestral and unceded Territory and Land of the Indigenous Peoples who have lived and continue to live on it. It honors their enduring connection to the Land and shows respect for their history and rights.

2SLGBTQIA+:
An acronym that stands for the terms Two-Spirit, Lesbian, Gay, Bisexual, Transgender, Queer or Questioning, Intersex, Asexual and other identities on the spectrum of gender identities and sexual orientations.

ACTION FOUR: *DON'T* Be a Performative Ally

THE SITUATION: Empty Words?

Each week in Kai's seventh grade classroom, the teacher asks a different student to start off Monday morning with a land acknowledgment—a statement acknowledging that the land a person is on is the Traditional Territory of specific Indigenous Peoples.

So far, several students have recited the words the teacher has written up on the white board: "I acknowledge the land of the Indigenous Peoples who first resided here." The whole class listens as the student stands up at their desk to speak, and then the student sits down and the teacher introduces their first lesson for the day.

Kai has listened attentively each week to the words spoken. They're sometimes left with questions, but since no one else raises their hands to say anything after the acknowledgment, Kai isn't sure they should either.

Kai knows a few things about Indigenous Peoples and their relationship with the land—they remember going on a nature walk with an Indigenous Elder in fifth grade, where the class learned about plants native to the area and how some Indigenous people use these plants for ceremonies and medicines. Kai has heard their parents talk about some of the ways the government has harmed Indigenous people, including by displacing them and taking control of their Traditional Lands and Territories. And Kai has heard land acknowledgments shared before other events they've attended, like when their family attended the Pride Festival last June. But some of those land acknowledgments sounded a little different from the one Kai's class recites.

As Kai's turn on Monday approaches, they're starting to feel uncomfortable and nervous, and they're not quite sure why. Something about this classroom practice just doesn't feel right, and Kai is starting to dread doing it.

Can you think of any reasons why Kai might be feeling the way they do?

Kai might be sensing several things here. The fact that they have questions about the land acknowledgment but don't feel there's room to ask those questions might signal to Kai that learning is not the priority in this particular instance, which might also seem strange to Kai, given that this is a classroom!

> Allyship is not self-defined—our work and our efforts must be recognized by the people we seek to ally ourselves with.

Layla Saad, author and activist

Kai also has had some prior experiences that suggest there is more to think about here. They know that land acknowledgments can look and sound different, and that might make Kai question why those differences exist, and why the land acknowledgment they use in their class sounds quite vague compared to others they've heard. Kai's experience going on the nature walk with an Indigenous Elder and interacting with the land could signal to them that acknowledging the land goes beyond mere words. And some of those conversations Kai has overheard their parents having might feel serious and important in a way they can't fully grasp but still perceive on some level.

Kai might not know precisely why they feel uncomfortable about what's going on in their classroom, but their discomfort is still real and important, and it's worth exploring further. Let's help Kai do that!

Read through "Authentic Allyship" versus "Performative Allyship" on the facing page. After reading, do any items feel particularly relevant in this situation? Might any of these statements help Kai navigate their feelings and how to proceed? Do you have any suggestions for Kai as the date for their land acknowledgment approaches?

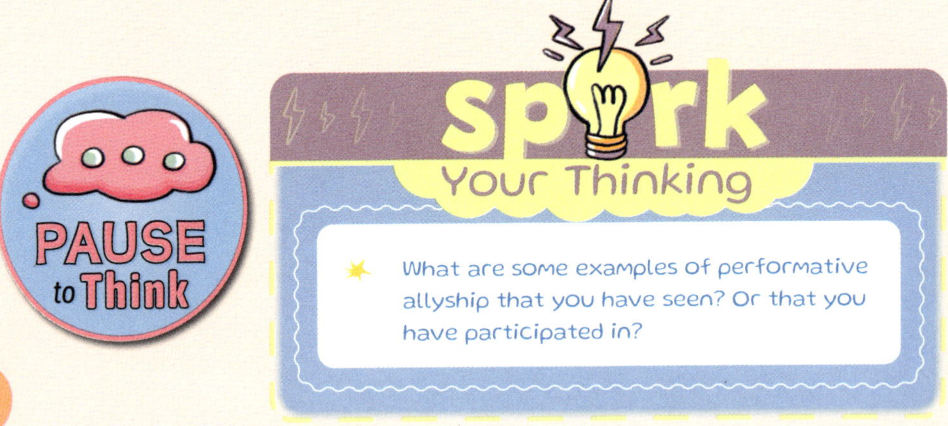

Am I Practicing Allyship or Performing It?

Authentic Allyship

- I take time to reflect on my privileges.
- I use my privileges to make room for others.
- I push myself to act when action is necessary.
- I expect and sit with discomfort.
- I make this work about benefitting others, not about making myself look good.
- I know allyship is an act that requires ongoing engagement.
- I act in allyship even when no one is going to know.
- I continue my learning.

Performative Allyship

- I don't really spend time learning or reflecting on my privileges or where others may be marginalized.
- I am concerned with appearances more than making a positive difference for others.
- I only show allyship when I benefit too.
- I center myself in conversations and actions.
- I "jump on the bandwagon" but do not commit for the long term.
- If called out, I respond with defensiveness or self-pity rather than open-mindedness and self-reflection.
- I make sure people know when I act in allyship.

LOOKING GOOD ISN'T ENOUGH

Performative allyship is when a person is more concerned with looking like they're doing the right thing than with challenging inequality or injustice. They might go through the motions, but people who "perform" allyship do little or nothing to actually create meaningful change.

Kai is starting to sense that the land acknowledgment their class recites every Monday is performative. No learning or reflection accompanies this act. The land acknowledgment seems more like a checkbox to be ticked off, or something to do because others are doing it, rather than a meaningful act in the service of others. No one who is Indigenous is benefitting from this land acknowledgment. In other words, the reflection, listening and learning, and action discussed in earlier chapters are all missing from this scenario.

What are some ways Kai could approach this situation?

Talking to someone would be a good start! Maybe Kai could share their feelings and questions about the land acknowledgment with their parents or a friend. This might help clarify some things and provide ways to proceed.

Kai could also spend a little time on their own learning about land acknowledgments—what are their purposes, how are they helpful (or not), and what could be included in one to make it more meaningful? Kai isn't too young to do some research!

Another, harder thing Kai could do is share their research and learning with their teacher and ask to share it with the class, too, as part of their own land acknowledgment on Monday. They could attach an invitation to further learning or action to their land acknowledgment as well. Sharing one's learning can be helpful in creating awareness, getting others to think about their actions and assumptions, and creating change. Would that be hard for a young person? Most definitely! But remember, action is important to allyship, and acting as an ally will almost always include some discomfort.

COMPLICATING THINGS EVEN MORE!

Let's add some more complexity to this conversation. Is sharing a land acknowledgment at the beginning of an event on its own ever enough? Is it possible that merely acknowledging the Indigenous territories one is on (or wearing a pink shirt for anti-bullying, or posting a Pride/rainbow flag on a store window, or adding your pronouns to your email signature) can make some kind of impact on its own, or is this just a performative action?

Personally, I love seeing rainbows around a school, signaling that the school is a safe space for 2SLGBTQIA+ people. Rainbow signage makes me feel more welcome...at least for a little while. But if the school doesn't match its actions to that statement, the welcome wears out for me. A land acknowledgment might do something similar—it can show Indigenous Peoples that non-Indigenous people are thinking about them and that they recognize Indigenous Peoples have a longstanding and integral relationship to the land, which can feel supportive. But if the people making those land acknowledgments aren't also taking action to make the lives of Indigenous Peoples better, that's not allyship! Allyship is continual, action-oriented and often uncomfortable.

"[Allyship] means not supporting something just because all of your friends are, but [...] because it's what **you** think is right."

Ash, age 12

"When I think of allyship, I think of helping someone out, even if there's nothing in return."

Avery, age 11

"Acting as an ally means not just saying you're an ally to make yourself look good but actually putting in effort to demand equality for people who lack some of the privileges you have."

Nero, age 13

ACTION FIVE: *DON'T* Assume

THE SITUATION: To Act or Not to Act?

Remember when I said action is key to being a strong ally? Well, sometimes action can look like listening and *not* acting. Weird, right? Here's what I mean.

Yifan is a fierce protector of her friends and family. She always sticks up for her little brother if others pick on him, and if anyone tries to insult her friends—even in a jokey way—Yifan says something.

One day at recess, Yifan, who is female, light-skinned and of Chinese ancestry, and her friend Riley, who's female, dark-skinned and of Nigerian ancestry, are outside kicking a ball around. A couple of kids start hovering nearby and begin to make rude comments about the girls' soccer skills. Then the kids' comments turn to racist insults about Riley's dark skin.

Yifan is angry! She tells the kids, "Leave Riley alone." But the kids keep taunting Riley, asking her why she isn't playing basketball instead of soccer, since she's Black. Yifan is about to say something, but Riley tells her to just leave it alone. She tries to pull Yifan away from the kids. But Yifan isn't having it—this is her friend!

WORDS to KNOW

Bystander: A person who witnesses an incident of bullying or harm but does not step in to help.

Upstander: Someone who takes action in situations of bullying or violence.

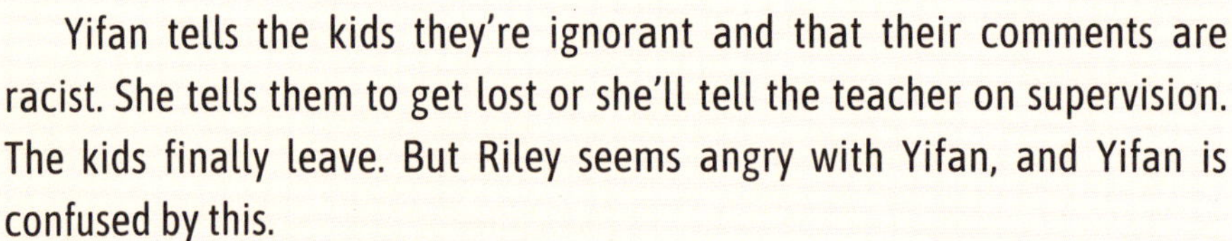

Yifan tells the kids they're ignorant and that their comments are racist. She tells them to get lost or she'll tell the teacher on supervision. The kids finally leave. But Riley seems angry with Yifan, and Yifan is confused by this.

Why might Riley be angry at Yifan?

WHAT TO DO?

Remember when I said allyship is a messy, tricky business? Well, here's a good example of that! Yifan is a good friend. She cares about Riley and wants to protect Riley from the kids who are bullying her. She takes action, like a good ally should. So what could possibly be problematic here?

Sometimes we have to listen and observe carefully to decide when and how to act as an ally. If Yifan really wants to act in Riley's best interests in this scenario, she might pay a bit more attention to Riley's cues—her request that Yifan leave things alone and her attempts to physically pull Yifan away. Instead of assuming that she knows best in this scenario, Yifan might trust that Riley knows what is best for herself.

But wouldn't that have just made Yifan a bystander? A bystander is someone who sees someone else being bullied or treated unjustly and doesn't do anything about it. In this scenario, Yifan was an upstander, someone who does their best to support and protect their peers. Yifan did what she thought was right in the situation, but could she have supported and protected her friend Riley in a different way while also respecting Riley's wishes?

You're not expected to become an expert, and there definitely won't be a test, but it's good to understand what people around you might be going through, so you can support them.

Lizzie Huxley-Jones, author

- Do you still have questions or concerns about this situation? If so, this could be a great time to chat with someone about them.
- How does it feel to know that sometimes allyship might actually mean ***not*** doing or saying something in a situation where someone is being treated unfairly?
- To push your thinking even further, consider this: Both Yifan and Riley could experience marginalization and racism based on their racial identities. But how might their experiences of racism differ? Why might it be important to note these differences?

OBSERVE and RESPECT

One possibility could be for Yifan to walk away with Riley, if that's what Riley wanted in the moment. Perhaps once they walked away, Yifan could have asked Riley what she wanted to happen next, if anything. Maybe Yifan could have simply said to the other kids, "This isn't right," and then walked away with Riley.

But what if the bullying continued—either that day or the next or the next? And what if Riley is too scared to say anything or let Yifan say anything? What should Yifan do then? How will she know when to listen to Riley's requests to leave it alone and when to say something?

Tricky business! If Riley's safety is at risk, Yifan should definitely tell someone, even if Riley doesn't want her to. Yifan might have to manage Riley's hurt or angry feelings after, but Riley's safety should come first.

Sometimes we have to listen to our friends and what they want and need in the moment. Sometimes an ally's best action is to listen carefully and pay attention to what someone wants and then do that thing.

Being an ally means anticipating when someone may need support. It's about understanding the power dynamics within a room.

Naomi and Natalie Evans,
authors and founders
of *Everyday Racism*

TRUSTING OTHERS and OURSELVES

Why wouldn't Riley have wanted Yifan to speak up for her in that moment?

Maybe Riley didn't want to be caught in the middle of the taunts and Yifan's defenses.

Maybe Riley knew those kids and knew that the more Yifan defended Riley, the more they would continue to bully her.

Maybe Riley was worried that if Yifan continued to defend her, things would escalate and get worse.

Maybe Riley felt that Yifan had assumed Riley couldn't defend herself simply because she chose not to say anything or react.

Whatever the reason, sometimes it's important as allies to simply trust that people know what is best for themselves—especially in the heat of a moment. It's not always easy to know when to step in and when not to. It's not easy to let people be treated unkindly or unfairly, even if they're asking us to walk away. It's not always easy to know if someone even means what they're saying or is just scared or tired!

Being an ally is not easy in so many ways. But as allies, it's important to struggle with these gray areas and do the best we can with the information we have in the moment. And understand that sometimes we might make mistakes, but that's part of allyship too.

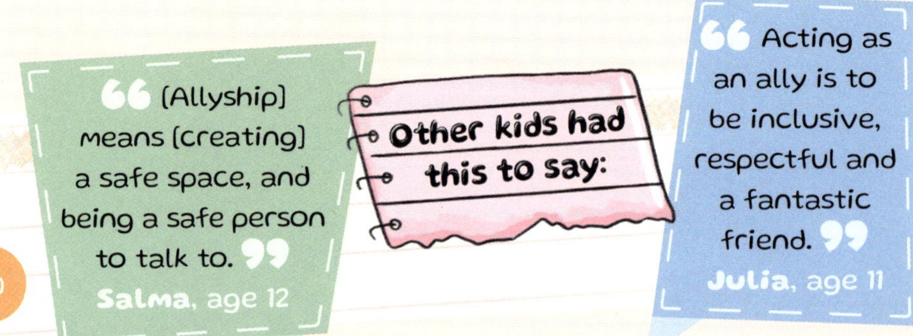

ACTION SIX: *DO* Be Ready for Mistakes and Saying "I'm Sorry"

THE SITUATION: Willing to Make It Right, Willing to Be Wrong

Consider the previous scenario with Yifan and Riley. Remember how Riley was angry with Yifan after their encounter with the two students who were bullying Riley? How does she go about repairing her relationship with Riley?

Acting in allyship will almost always lead to discomfort and mistakes. Challenging ourselves to be better in some way will require going outside of our comfort zones, which means things will be hard sometimes and we'll make mistakes.

WORDS to KNOW

Intention: What someone means to do.

Impact: The results of someone's actions.

Microaggression: A slight, subtle discriminatory comment or action that shows negativity toward marginalized groups. It may be unintentional, but it can still hurt people and make them feel bad.

WHAT WOULD YOU DO IN THESE SCENARIOS?

- You accidentally use she/her pronouns for someone who identifies as nonbinary and uses they/them pronouns. What do you do in the moment? What do you do afterward? What do you *not* do?
- You ask a friend's cousin, who has brown skin but was born in the same city as you, where they are from. Your friend later tells you that this was a microaggression, and it made your friend angry. What do you do in the moment? What do you do afterward? What do you *not* do?

So part of being a good ally is also learning how to address mistakes when we make them. What could Yifan do in this scenario?

If you said "apologize," that is a great start! Once Yifan realizes she's hurt her friend, even if she didn't mean to, she can apologize. If you were Yifan, how might you word your apology?

Some possibilities:

"I realized I didn't listen to what you were telling me at recess, and I'm sorry."

"I'm sorry if I said something you didn't want me to say in front of those kids."

"I was trying to help, but I think I made you mad instead. I'm really sorry. I'll try my best to do better next time."

You might be thinking, But Yifan was just trying to help. Why should she apologize for trying her best to be a good ally?

Fair question! Let's make an important distinction: the difference between intentions and impact. We might have all the best *intentions*, but if our actions end up having a negative *impact* on people, an apology can do a lot to reduce that negative impact. When apologizing, try to think more about the impact you made rather than your intentions. Focus on how the other person might be feeling. It can be a powerful gesture to take responsibility for your impact on others and—if that impact is negative in some way—to apologize for the harm you caused.

> **What if I make a mistake? Racism is a volatile issue, and I don't want to say or do the wrong thing.** In almost 40 years of teaching and leading workshops about racism, I have made many mistakes. I have found that a sincere apology and a genuine desire to learn from one's mistakes is usually rewarded with forgiveness. If we wait for perfection, we will never break the silence. The cycle of racism will continue uninterrupted.

Beverly Daniel Tatum,
author, educator
and psychologist

What if Riley is still angry with Yifan, even after Yifan apologizes? What should Yifan do then?

One possibility is to accept that Riley might need more time to process Yifan's apology before accepting it, so Yifan might need to give Riley a bit of space at this stage. In the meantime, Yifan can pay attention to Riley's needs, continue to listen and continue to learn. Some things Yifan might want to avoid are pressing Riley to accept her apology, getting angry with Riley for not accepting the apology and not learning from her own mistakes.

"[Allyship] is really having someone's back from start to end."
Eliza, age 12

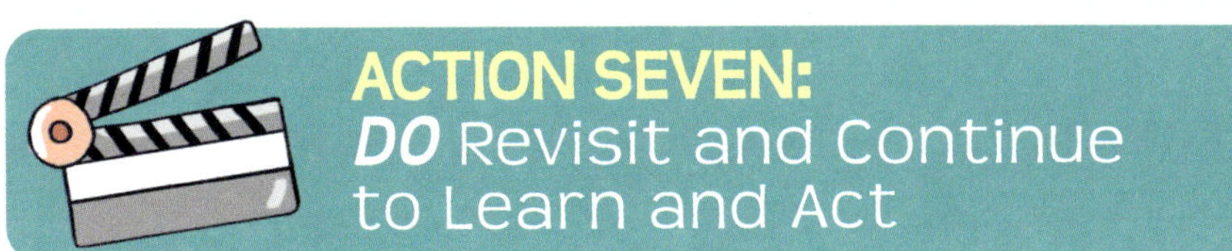

ACTION SEVEN: *DO* Revisit and Continue to Learn and Act

THE SITUATION: You. Here. Now.

Maybe, as you're learning about allyship, it's starting to feel overwhelming. There's a lot to know and many opportunities to make mistakes. It seems like a lot of work, time and effort. It also feels like things are constantly changing, and you'll never know everything.

Or perhaps you're excited to practice what you've learned, even if you know you'll make some mistakes along the way and there will be times when you don't know what to do.

Or you might be feeling something in between. Whatever those feelings are, they're natural and okay.

What is truly important, though, is that you find a way to move forward. If you're excited, that won't be much of a problem. But if you're overwhelmed or scared or frustrated or unsure, it may feel easier to just keep doing what you've been doing, or ignore these issues altogether, or run and hide when difficult situations come up.

So how do we keep going? Following are three practical strategies:

REMINDERS

Find a favorite resource—a book (maybe it's this one!), a video, an article, a few quotes—that inspires you toward allyship, and keep it close to your heart and mind. Come back to it every few weeks or months. Use it to remind yourself that allyship requires reflecting on yourself and the people around you, that it requires action, that it involves mistakes and apologies. Check in with yourself using questions such as:

- What else do I need to learn?
- In what ways do I have more freedom than others have?
- Where might I be leaving people out?
- How is my allyship helping people? Or is it?

GOALS

Identifying one or two key goals for yourself around allyship could help make this work more manageable and less overwhelming for you. What is a goal that will help you become a consistent, active ally? Maybe it's a simple one to start, or maybe you're ready for something a little more challenging. Try coming up with one or two right now!

Some Possible Goals

- I'm going to follow [a particular account] on YouTube and watch at least one video per week that it produces.
- I'm going to practice listening by waiting until at least one person from a marginalized group has spoken before sharing my own ideas in class discussions.
- The next time my [family member] says something harmful about [a particular group of people], I'm going to ask them why they think that and then share what I think, even if it feels super awkward.

It's important to revisit goals as well. Maybe post your goal somewhere that will remind you of it daily or weekly.

3 BUDDIES

Making progress can be more powerful in pairs or groups, because we have someone to cheer us on, discuss our messy thoughts with, learn from and hold us accountable to our goals.

Is there someone you can speak with about the ups and downs of allyship? Someone who will help motivate you to continue this learning and work? You don't have to form a book club or study group or anything like that (although no one's stopping you!), but maybe you and a friend can plan to talk about the hard stuff when it comes up, ask questions of each other with no judgment or share resources with each other. Or maybe you could join a group at school, such as a Gender and Sexuality Alliance or social justice club, that discusses these kinds of things.

> The aim of this work is truth—seeing it, owning it and figuring out what to do with it. This is lifelong work. Avoid the shortcuts, and be wary of the easy answers.

Layla Saad, author and activist

Each person, human or no, is bound to every other in a reciprocal relationship. Just as all beings have a duty to me, I have a duty to them...An integral part of a human's education is to know those duties and how to perform them.

Robin Wall Kimmerer,
author and scientist

There's certainly time for quiet, reflective, personal learning, but going beyond our own brains and feelings can also help us grow in unexpected and wonderful ways.

If I've learned anything about allyship, it's that being an ally takes time, patience and continual learning. It can't be summed up in any one resource or by any one person. There are plenty of people who can offer you great suggestions as well, so head to the Resources section for more options!

Plan for Action

Come up with a small plan of action now by filling in the blanks.

- One way I'll remind myself of what I've learned here is...
- One goal I have is...
- Someone I can ask to be my partner in learning is...
- A resource I'm going to read/watch/listen to is...

MY GRATITUDE TO YOU!

Did I mention how proud I am of you for being here? Well, I am. It takes something special to devote your precious time and energy to learning about allyship. If you've made it through this book, then I have faith that you're going to contribute something valuable to others, and I thank you in advance! A world filled with young people like you is one I want to live in, and I feel lucky to have spent this bit of time with you.

Other kids had this to say:

"An ally is someone who is there for people who really need them."
Gemma, age 11

"Acting as an ally means supporting and not judging people who are trying to be who they are or want to be."
Taylor, age 13

Resources

PRINT

Bourne, Shakirah, and Dana Alison Levy, eds. *Allies: Real Talk about Showing Up, Screwing Up, and Trying Again*. DK Children, an imprint of PRH, 2021.

Johnson, Chelsea, LaToya Council and Carolyn Choi. *Intersection Allies: We Make Room for All*. Dottir Press, 2019.

Kimmerer, Robin Wall, and Monique Gray Smith. *Braiding Sweetgrass for Young Adults: Indigenous Wisdom, Scientific Knowledge, and the Teachings of Plants*. Zest Books, an imprint of Lerner Publishing Group, 2022.

Oluo, Ijeoma. *So You Want to Talk about Race*. Seal Press, 2018.

Wong, Alice, ed. *Disability Visibility (Adapted for Young Adults): 17 First-Person Stories for Today*. Ember, an imprint of Penguin Random House, 2023.

ONLINE

Canadian Centre for Diversity and Inclusion, Glossary of Terms: ccdi.ca/media/3150/ccdi-glossary-of-terms-eng.pdf

Code Switch (podcast): npr.org/podcasts/510312/codeswitch

Disability in Kidlit: disabilityinkidlit.com

Facing History and Ourselves: facinghistory.org

How to Be A Good Ally: Identity, Privilege, Resistance: youtube.com/watch?v=q7ElX4GFQpI

Indigenous Ally Toolkit: reseaumtlnetwork.com/wp-content/uploads/2022/12/Ally_March.pdf

National Centre for Truth and Reconciliation: nctr.ca

Privilege Explained for Kids: youtube.com/watch?v=qfCwwc1mqKw

Rainbow Book List: glbtrt.ala.org/rainbowbooks

Social Justice Books: socialjusticebooks.org

The Gender Unicorn: youtube.com/watch?v=YPNCzXYy2CE

The Secret Life of Canada (podcast): cbc.ca/radio/secretlifeofcanada

The Trevor Project: Guide to Being an Ally to Transgender and Nonbinary Young People: thetrevorproject.org/resources/guide/a-guide-to-being-an-ally-to-transgender-and-nonbinary-youth

We Need Diverse Books: diversebooks.org

Acknowledgments

Thanks so much to my editor, Kirstie Hudson at Orca, for inviting and encouraging me to try out a nonfiction book for middle grades, which is completely out of my wheelhouse! I gained a lot from the experience. Big gratitude to Orca Book Publishers and its whole team as well, who I've admired for so long and am thrilled to be working with on this book. Special thanks to Ruth Linka and Tara Solomon for their guidance and support. To Bithi Sutradhar, thank you for your lively and careful illustrations! Thank you also to Robin Stevenson for lending me her valuable insight because this *is* her wheelhouse, and I trust her wisdom. Thank you to the sensitivity readers who provided such caring, thoughtful feedback: Chanelle Tye, Zuri Scrivens and Jennifer Sharpe. Thanks to all the kids who gifted me their sage tips and ideas about allyship—kids are so smart, and I'm always thrilled to learn from them. In fact, I've learned about allyship from a lot of people, some of whom I refer to in this book and on the resource pages. I hope I've done them and the topic justice. And I'd be remiss if I didn't thank all the people who have been incredible allies to this queer brown girl over the years, putting aside their own discomfort to make space for me and my communities. Hands up to you! And, finally, I'm always grateful to my wife, Jennifer, who's a powerful ally in so many ways to the people around her.

Index

Jennifer Ivings

TANYA BOTEJU is a teacher and writer living on unceded territories of the Musqueam, Squamish and Tsleil-Waututh First Nations (Vancouver, BC). Part-time she teaches English to clever and sassy young people. The rest of her time, she uses writing as an excuse to eat pastries. Her debut novel, *Kings, Queens, and In-Betweens* (Simon & Schuster, 2019), was named a Top Ten Indie Next pick by the American Booksellers Association. A second book, *Bruised* (Simon & Schuster, 2021), was selected as a Gold Standard book by the Junior Library Guild. Look for her next YA novel, *Messy Perfect*, in 2025. As an educator committed to anti-oppressive teaching and learning, and as an imperfect ally herself, she hopes her books bend the universe even the tiniest bit toward justice. Visit her at tanyaboteju.com.

BITHI SUTRADHAR is a Bangladeshi illustrator and graphic designer who holds a master of publishing degree from Simon Fraser University, as well as an MFA and BFA in graphic design from the University of Dhaka. Alongside her professional illustration work, Bithi enjoys sharing her knowledge and skills through teaching. Her contributions have been recognized by educational institutions and government bodies such as the Ministry of Agriculture in Bangladesh. In 2024, Bithi created the illustrations for the first three books in the Take Action series as part of an internship with Orca Book Publishers. Bithi lives in Vancouver and loves exploring the vibrant outdoor scenes in her spare time, finding inspiration in the city's natural beauty.

Anik Saha

DO TAKE
DO REFLECT ON THE SIMILARITIES AND DIFFERENCES BETWEEN YOURSELF AND OTHERS
DO ACT IN THE MOMENT
DO CONTINUALLY LISTEN AND LEARN
DON'T BE A PERFORMATIVE ALLY